# EILEEN DIAMOND
# MUSICAL PLAYS 2
## FOR JUNIOR SCHOOLS

## Contents

*\* New edition by the composer*

First Published 1989
© Chappell Music Ltd
129 Park Street, London W1Y 3FA

Exclusive Distributors
International Music Publications
Southend Road, Woodford Green,
Essex IG8 8HN, England.

1-2-51125

# The Sad King

Words and Music by
EILEEN DIAMOND

## List of Characters

KING
1st GIRL
2nd GIRL
3rd GIRL
THREE SERVANTS

Solo parts

Action only

CHORUS

Any number

## Props

'Jewellery and Pearls' for 1st GIRL.
Large 'diamond' brooch for 2nd GIRL.
(This can be made out of cardboard, glue and silver glitter).
White 'wedding dress' and veil for 3rd GIRL.

The GIRLS wait off stage. CHORUS stand at the back of the stage.
In front of them, the THREE SERVANTS stand to one side.

## Action

While the CHORUS sing the first verse, the KING walks up and down centre stage. He looks very sad and makes occasional loud sighs.

At the words 'He sent all his courtiers' the KING beckons to the SERVANTS and points, directing them off stage. The SERVANTS exit and return with the three GIRLS, who curtsey to the KING and stand to one side. The SERVANTS move to the opposite side of the stage.

After the KING sings his solo 'I wonder why you yearn' etc., the 1st GIRL steps forward and curtseys before singing her solo, pointing to the jewels. The KING sings again, and the 1st GIRL returns to her place. The CHORUS sing and the KING walks and sighs as before.

The 2nd GIRL steps forward, curtseys before singing and points to large diamond brooch at appropriate words. She points her finger at KING for 'I'd keep a strict eye on you', the KING reacts as for 1st GIRL.

The 3rd GIRL steps forward and curtseys. The KING now looks very sad and keeps his head down until CHORUS sing 'The King raised his head'. He smiles, and holds out his hands. He sings 'Please marry me', the GIRL nods her head. They exit together.

The CHORUS sing 'Oh King' etc., during which the GIRL makes a quick change into her dress and veil. (The music slows down before the Wedding March to allow more time).

The KING and his Queen enter and wal round the stage hand in hand, they kiss centre stage and stand looking happy.

# The Sad King

Words and Music by
EILEEN DIAMOND

**Gently and not too fast.**

*Chorus* The King walked a - lone in his pal - ace, he had
sent all his ser - vants out search - ing, they

ne - ver been so un - hap - py in his life, for al - though he was a King, and
found the pret - ti - est girls to be seen, but the King had a task, each

he had ev - ery - thing, he just could - n't find him - self a wife.
girl he had to ask, to tell him why she want - ed to be Queen.

*poco rit.*

4

this is what he said: *King:* "I'm ve - ry sor - ry dear but you won't do."

*{1st Girl} {2nd Girl} walk sadly back*

*poco rit*

*a tempo*

*Chorus* Poor King, sad King, he'd nev-er been so un-hap-py in his life.

*{2nd Girl} {3rd Girl} moves forward and curtseys*

Poor King sad un-hap-py King, the on-ly thing he want-ed was a wife. *2nd Girl* "Oh

8

# The Sad King

**Words and Music by
EILEEN DIAMOND**

CHORUS

The King walked alone in his palace,
He had never been so unhappy in his life,
For although he was King, and he had everything,
He just couldn't find himself a wife.

Poor King, sad King,
He'd never been so unhappy in his life.
Poor King, sad unhappy King,
The only thing he wanted was a wife.

He sent all his servants out searching,
They found the prettiest girls to be seen,
But the King had a task, each girl he had to ask
To tell him why she wanted to be Queen.

Poor King, sad King,
He'd never been so unhappy in his life.
Poor King, sad unhappy King,
The only thing he wanted was a wife.

KING

The King asked each in turn:
"Please tell me why you yearn
To come and be my Queen and marry me?"
*(1st GIRL steps forward and curtseys)*

1st GIRL

"Oh I'd like to wear lots of jewellery
And I'd like to wear lots of pearls,
I'd so like to be very different you see
And not just like all other girls".

CHORUS

The King shook his head,
And this is what he said:

KING

"I'm very sorry dear but you won't do".
*(1st GIRL walks slowly back)*

CHORUS

Poor King, sad King,
He'd never been so unhappy in his life.
Poor King, sad unhappy King
The only thing he wanted was a wife.

2nd GIRL

"Oh I'd like to give lots of orders,
And tell people what they have to do,
I'd ride in your coach, wear a big diamond brooch,
And I'd keep a strict eye on you!"

CHORUS

The King shook his head,
And this is what he said:

KING

"I'm very sorry dear but you won't do".
*(2nd GIRL walks slowly back)*

CHORUS

Poor King, sad King,
He'd never been so happy in his life.
Poor King, sad unhappy King
The only thing he wanted was a wife.

*3rd GIRL*  "Oh I'd like to visit the people,
And help them as much as I can,
But my main aim in life, is to be a better wife,
And make you a very happy man."

*CHORUS*  The King raised his head,
And this is what he said:

*KING*  "At last I've found true love, please marry me."
*(King takes 3rd GIRL by the hand and they exit.)*

*CHORUS*  Oh King, happy happy King,
At last he found the love he'd waited for.
Oh King, happy happy King,
He would not be unhappy anymore.
*(King and bride enter after wedding march.)*

And then came the day they were married,
The King took his bride by the hand,
They kissed tenderly, and it was plain to see,
He was the happiest man in all the land.

Oh King, happy happy King,
He'd never been so happy in his life.
Oh King, happy happy King,
At last he has found himself a wife.

# The Toy Shop

### Words and Music by
### EILEEN DIAMOND

## List of Characters

THE TOYMAKER
RAG DOLL
SOLDIER                        Solo parts
CLOWN
FAIRY DOLL

(Other children may be dressed up as toys and join in the action, if wished)

CHORUS                         Any number

## Musical Instruments

CUCKOO CLOCK      C and A chime bars or metallophone
WHISTLE           Whistle or recorder
BELL              Hand bell
TELEPHONE         Rapidly played triangle

## Props and Costumes

For the Toymaker: Nightshirt or pyjama top, slippers, work bag, duvet or
                  blanket and pillow for bed.

Appropriate clothes for the TOYS
Any children's toys to sit around the toy shop. A doll's tea set,
conveniently placed. A screen would be effective to divide the
TOYMAKER's bedroom from the shop, (but it is not essential).

The CHORUS stand backstage; in front of them to one side, stand the
four musical instrument players; on the other side is the TOYMAKER's
bed.
The TOYMAKER stands centre-stage with his bag open on the floor.
The four TOYS sit on the floor in front of him. Other toys stand nearby.

# Action

The triangle player strikes six times. After a slight pause, the introduction begins and the CHORUS starts to sing. The TOYMAKER performs appropriate actions and waves to his toys as he says good-night. He moves over to his bedroom, takes off his slippers and lies down.
When the whistle blows for the third time at the end of the chorus, the TOYMAKER sits up in bed and puts his hand to his ear to sing 'Did I hear a noise?' etc. At the words 'Oh, no', he shakes his head, makes hand actions pretending to turn out the light, waves good-night again to the toys and folds his arms firmly at the words, 'So it must be all right. He lies down again. When the CHORUS sing 'But the toys had decided to play', the TOYS stand up and sing their parts. They form a line behind the SOLDIER and march around while the instruments play; they stand still when the CHORUS sing 'The toymaker said as he sat up in bed'.

The TOYMAKER sits up and makes the same hand actions as previously, before lying back on the bed again.

The CLOWN begins a polka at the words 'One, two and three, hop' and beckons to the other toys to join him. They all dance the polka while the instruments play; then they sit down on the floor.

Towards the end of the chorus, the TOYMAKER sits up listening, gets out of bed and kneels down with his ear to the ground. He stands up and repeats the previous actions. After the words 'But I think I'd better see', he puts on his slippers and begins moving towards the shop, timing his actions to arrive just after the TOYS whisper good-night.

Meanwhile, the TOYS pretend to drink tea and perform the other actions. They whisper good-night to each other, close their eyes, and pretend to be asleep.

The TOYMAKER arrives centre-stage and sings his part 'Those noises I heard', etc.

The TOYS sit up and wink at each other, then stand up. The TOYMAKER moves towards them and all dance freely to the final chorus.

# The Toy Shop

Words and Music by
EILEEN DIAMOND

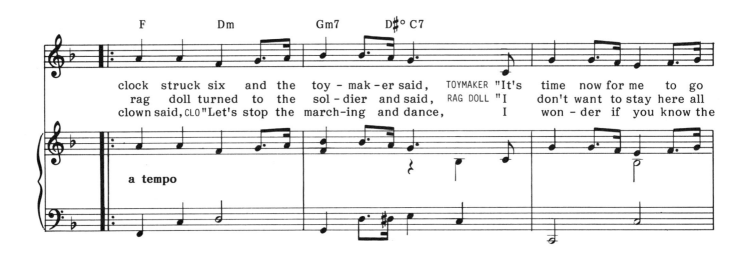

18

# The Princess Who Couldn't Make Up Her Mind

Words and Music by
EILEEN DIAMOND

## List of Characters

PRINCESS ⎫
KING ⎪
1st PRINCE ⎬ Solo singing parts
2nd PRINCE ⎪
3rd PRINCE ⎭
NARRATOR                     Solo speaking part

CHORUS                    Any number

## Props

Large written sign: THREE WEEKS LATER
Three empty flower pots
Bottle for perfume
Toy beads for jewellery
Crumpled black paper or earth to fill third pot
(The seed may be imaginary — or use large bead or plum stone.)

The CHORUS stand around the back of the room or stage. In front of
them, the three PRINCES stand on one side, the PRINCESS stands
central stage and the KING on the other side.
The NARRATOR waits off stage, or may be one of the CHORUS.

## Action

As the PRINCES sing 'I do so hope' etc. each one in turn takes a step
forward. The PRINCESS steps forward to sing 'Oh dear, oh dear' etc.
putting a hand up to her head to express bewilderment. During the dance
interludes between the verses, the PRINCESS takes the hands of each
PRINCE in turn and dances round once with each one, then moves back
to central stage. At the beginning of the second verse she moves over to
the KING. The NARRATOR walks to front central stage speaks his part
and exits.
The KING fetches three pots and gives one to each PRINCE, then points
to off-stage dismissing the three PRINCES who exit. NARRATOR returns
holding up THREE WEEKS LATER sign and exits.
The PRINCES return with their pots appropriately filled, each one
covered with a paper bag. Each PRINCE uncovers his pot when he sings
'See what I have here'. The pots are placed on the floor while the
PRINCES dance. For the final dance, the PRINCESS dances only with the
third PRINCE.

# The Princess Who Couldn't Make Up Her Mind

Words and Music by
EILEEN DIAMOND

# The Princess Who Couldn't Make Up Her Mind

**Words and Music by**
**EILEEN DIAMOND**

| | |
|---|---|
| *CHORUS* | There was once a very pretty princess,<br>She was fair and she was good.<br>There were once three handsome princes,<br>Who would marry her if they could. |
| *1st PRINCE* | 'Oh I am hoping she will marry me'. |
| *2nd PRINCE* | 'And I am hoping she will marry me'. |
| *3nd PRINCE* | 'And I am hoping she will marry me'. |
| *PRINCESS* | 'Oh dear oh dear! Now which one shall it be?' |
| *CHORUS* | She just couldn't make up her mind. |
| | *(Dance)* |
| *CHORUS* | So she went to ask her father<br>Who was king of all the land, |
| *PRINCESS* | 'Father please could you advise me<br>To which prince shall I give my hand?' |
| *1st PRINCE* | 'Oh I am hoping she will marry me'. |
| *2nd PRINCE* | 'And I am hoping she will marry me'. |
| *3rd PRINCE* | 'And I am hoping she will marry me'. |
| *PRINCESS* | 'Oh dear oh dear! Now which one shall it be?' |
| *CHORUS* | She just couldn't make up her mind. |
| | *(Dance)* |
| *KING* | 'Yes I think I can advise you<br>As to which one you should choose,<br>And you princes have to realise<br>One must win and two must lose'. |
| *1st PRINCE* | 'Oh I am hoping she will marry me'. |
| *2nd PRINCE* | 'And I am hopinh she will marry me'. |
| *3rd PRINCE* | 'And I am hoping she will marry me'. |
| *PRINCESS* | 'Oh dear oh dear! Now which one shall it me?' |
| *CHORUS* | She just couldn't make up her mind. |
| | *(Dance)* |

| | |
|---|---|
| *NARRATOR* | The king then gave each prince an empty pot. He told the princes to go away and fill their pots with something that they thought would most please the princess, and to return and present it to her three weeks later. *(exit princes)* |
| | *(Holds up sign saying THREE WEEKS LATER. The Princes return with their pots).* |
| *1st PRINCE* | 'Oh princess dear see what I have here, All my money I have spent On something that I am sure you will like It's a beautiful bottle of scent. Oh I am hoping she will marry me'. |
| *2nd PRINCE* | 'And I am hoping she will marry me'. |
| *3rd PRINCE* | 'And I am hoping she will marry me'. |
| *PRINCESS* | 'I can't say now, you will have to wait and see'. |
| *CHORUS* | 'She just hadn't made up her mind'. |
| | *(Dance)* |
| *2nd PRINCE* | 'Oh princess dear see what I have here, Precious jewels of every kind, Some sapphires blue and some diamonds too This is sure to make up your mind'. |
| *1st PRINCE* | 'Oh I am hoping she will marry me'. |
| *2nd PRINCE* | 'And I am hoping she will marry me'. |
| *3rd PRINCE* | 'And I am hoping she will marry me'. |
| *PRINCESS* | 'I can't say now, you will have to wait and see'. |
| *CHORUS* | She just hadn't made up her mind. |
| | *(Dance)* |
| *3rd PRINCE* | 'Oh princess dear see what I have here I have filled my pot with earth'. |
| *1st PRINCE (horrified!)* | 'With earth! What an insult!' |
| *2nd PRINCE* | 'With earth! How does he dare!' |
| *KING (disbelieving)* | 'Just earth! I can't believe it, But wait! What does he have there?' |
| *3rd PRINCE* | 'Now in this pot here's a seed I'll sow Which is like my love for you, For every day you will watch it grow, It will give you pleasure too'. |

*1st PRINCE (with dismay)*
        'Oh dear! That's rather clever!'

*2nd PRINCE*      'Oh dear! That's rather good'.

*KING*              'Indeed, this man has something.
                    For the pot he has brought shows the greatest thought'.

*PRINCESS*      'Oh yes, I agree, he's the prince for me'.

*CHORUS*        She had suddenly made up her mind!

                *(Dance)*

# The Sleepy Mandarin

Words and Music by
EILEEN DIAMOND

## List of Characters

MANDARIN
4 AMBASSADORS    }        Solo singing parts
GIRL

4 SERVANTS

THE 'SOUND PLAYERS' (These parts may be doubled)
Drums
Bells    }        Any number of each
Claves

CHORUS  }
CITIZENS }        Any number

## Musical Instruments

GONG (Cymbal with beater)       BELLS (small handbells)
TRIANGLE                          SLEIGH BELLS
DRUMS                            CLAVES

## Props

Chair for the MANDARIN
Four pocket watches for the AMBASSADORS. (May be made out of cardboard hung on gold ribbon).

Two banners with large written letters, the first one saying:
COMPETITION
BRING A SOUND TO WAKE THE MANDARIN
The second one saying:
8 a.m. AT THE PALACE

## Costumes

The AMBASSADORS should wear coloured sashes. Chinese style costumes and make-up for all other characters.

# Action

The MANDARIN stands in front of a chair on one side of the stage attended by the SERVANTS (two on either side). Next to them stand the TRIANGLE, GONG, and SLEIGH BELL PLAYERS. The CHORUS stand on the other side of the stage.

When the CHORUS start to sing, the CITIZENS enter and file past the MANDARIN, bowing to him. He shakes hands with them and appears to counsel them, after which they exit and the MANDARIN sits down.

At the words 'But the Mandarin had a problem too' he 'falls asleep' and appears to be sleeping heavily (breathes deeply).

While the CHORUS sing, 'He was late' etc., the SERVANTS (gently!) shake him and try unsuccessfully to wake him. They sing 'Please will you wake up' urgently in his ears. The MANDARIN wakes up rubbing his eyes, stands to sing his part, then sits down and falls asleep again while the CHORUS sing 'He was late'.

When the AMBASSADORS enter, they look annoyed, and constantly look at their watches. After singing their parts they exit.

The SERVANTS sing 'Nicest possible sound', and also exit. They return holding the banners, walking round with them while singing. They exit again and return without banners to stand either side of the sleeping MANDARIN. The 'SOUND PLAYERS' and GIRL enter and stand centre stage. Each group in turn moves forward to play their 'Sound'.

The MANDARIN says 'That wouldn't get me out of bed' sleepily, dozes off again, and the 'SOUND PLAYERS' exit.

After the GIRL has sung her first refrain, the MANDARIN wakes and sits up listening interestedly, standing to sing 'That voice is much sweeter'. He falls asleep again after singing the words 'To get me out of bed'!

When the GIRL has sung her refrain, the AMBASSADORS again enter. The MANDARIN stands up and while the CHORUS sing, he greets the AMBASSADORS. During 'Has everybody heard?' the CITIZENS and 'SOUND PLAYERS' also enter. Everyone joins in the spoken words and sings the final chorus while the MANDARIN walks among them shaking hands. They bow as he passes.

Finally, he faces the GIRL, who bows to him; taking her hand, he bows to her.

# The Sleepy Mandarin

Words and Music by
EILEEN DIAMOND

36

43

# The Little Gingerbread Man

Words and Music by
EILEEN DIAMOND

## List of Characters

CHEF                                    Solo part
1st GINGERBREAD MAN ⎫
2nd GINGERBREAD MAN ⎬                    Action only
3rd GINGERBREAD MAN ⎭
4th GINGERBREAD MAN                      Solo part
QUEEN                                    Solo part

CHORUS                                   Any number

## Action

The CHORUS stand around the back of the stage or room.
In front of them, the CHEF, holding a rolling-pin, stands behind a low table.

The QUEEN waits off-stage.

Four children crouch down beside the CHEF. They are the 'pieces of dough' to become the four gingerbread men.

As the music starts, the CHEF takes the first piece of dough — this child lies on the table — and pretends to roll it with the rolling-pin.

The CHORUS point to mouth, eyes, arms, legs etc. as they sing about them. At the words, 'He's a lovely little gingerbread man', the child on the table gets up, and dances with the CHEF. This 1st GINGERBREAD MAN then stands to one side and the CHEF repeats the actions with the second and third pieces of dough, during the second and third verses.

The fourth verse is then enacted. At the words, 'He made one, two, three', the 4th GINGERBREAD MAN (the remaining piece of dough) points sadly to the other three GINGERBREAD MEN and at the end of his solo, crouches down once more.

The QUEEN enters and sings her part to the CHEF. When she has finished, on the cue 'there are four' the 4th GINGERBREAD MAN pops up to sing, 'what was that I heard, upon my word!' and crouches down again.

The CHEF makes the 4th GINGERBREAD MAN, and is then joined by the QUEEN and all four GINGERBREAD MEN for a final dance.

# The Little Gingerbread Man

Words and Music by
EILEEN DIAMOND

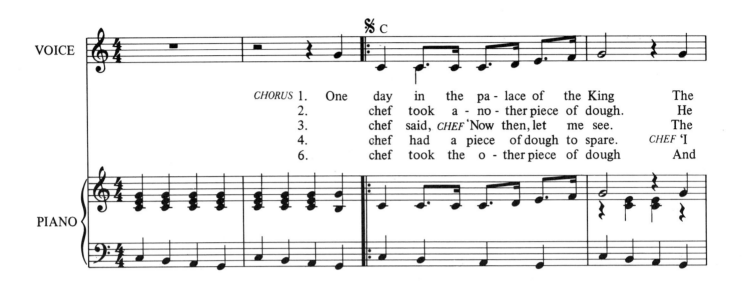

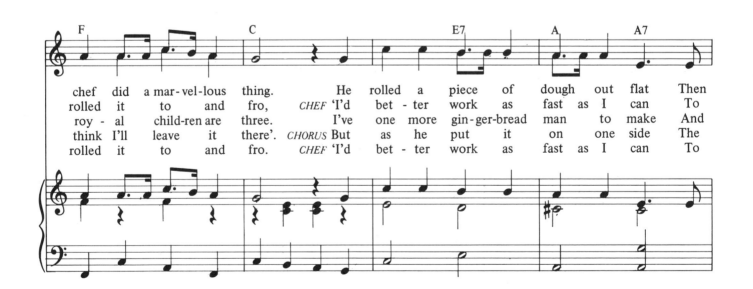